Have Your Cake & EAT IT TOO!

The Savvy & Sassy Guide to Get What
YOU Want in Life & Business

CHERYL HOLLAND

HAVE YOUR CAKE & EAT IT TOO!

Copyright ©2014 Cheryl Holland

All rights reserved. No part of this book may be reproduced or transmitted in any form or by any means, electronic or mechanical, except as permitted under Section 107 or 108 of the 1976 United States Copyright Act, without prior written consent of the publisher except for the inclusion of brief quotes in a review. While the author and publisher have used their best efforts in preparing this book, they make no representations or warranties with respect to the accuracy or completeness of the contents of this book.

ISBN: 978-0-692-26908-4
Printed in the United States of America

Book design and publishing
A'Sista Media Group, LLC
www.asistamedia .com

Cover Photo
Jeff Brooks Photography

This book is dedicated to my mother, Jennie Ann Orum, who raised me to be a woman of grace, poise and integrity. Her support, love, and prayers continue to carry me.

Thanks Ma for everything you do for me. I love you with all of my heart!

Cheryl

ACKNOWLEDGMENTS

With Special Thanks:
To my Lord and savior, thank You for everything that I am and that I have because without you I am and have nothing. I am forever grateful for the privilege of sharing what you have given me.

To my handsome sons, Brandon and Jourdan, I love you and hope that this book also inspires you to be the best that you can be.

To my aunts Loretta Cummings and Linda Barnes, thank you so much for always supporting and being the helping hands.

To my granddaughters Adrianna and Gabriella, this book is a legacy for you. I want you to believe that you can have anything that you want in this life. If Mimi can do it, so can you.

Thank you to my pastors, Bishop Rodney and Pastor Michelle Roberts. You have sown seeds into my life that will produce a tremendous harvest.

To all my special friends who have prayed for me and given me encouragement and support along the way, thank you from the bottom of my heart.

CONTENTS

Acknowledgements — 5
Foreword — 9
Introduction — 11

PART 1 - THE MAIN INGREDIENTS — 17

Chapter 1: The Right Ingredients — 19
Chapter 2: Knowing What You Want — 31
Chapter 3: Doing It With Intention — 43
Chapter 4: Put a Demand on Your Potential — 51

PART 2 - GET BAKED — 63

Chapter 5: Stay in the Oven — 65
Chapter 6: Create a Curb and Kick'em There — 71
Chapter 7: Get out of Your Own Way — 81

PART 3 - HAVING YOUR CAKE — 89

Chapter 8: Don't Throw Away the Crumbs — 91
Chapter 9: Treat People Like Icing — 99
Chapter 10: Brand You New — 105

FOREWORD

Ultimate living and creating a life that you want is what most people dream about. However, most get stuck and become frustrated and confused about how they can change their every day living so that they can finally move toward living the life of their dreams. Many women today spend their lives searching and hoping to achieve, acquire and accomplish but never reaching the success they really want. I'm convinced that true success is fulfilling every dream God has placed inside of you so that you can live at your fullest potential.

My own personal experience as a life and success coach has taught me that most people need help changing their thinking so they can change their habits to start living a higher life. I've coached Cheryl over the last two years and I've seen the growth in her own life and business.

In this powerful book, Cheryl, in her own savvy and sassy way helps you connect the dots with your inner life and your outer circumstances, grab the reins so you can take center stage in your own life and move from overwhelm and frustration to discover how to live a happy and purposeful life—having your cake and eating it too. Throughout the book, she shares her own personal process and creatively interweaves inspiring wisdom of experience and spiritual principles that will empower you to make a change for the better.

If you've been looking for a way to shift from where you are in your life now to where you really want to be, then I encourage you to start now with this book. One of my most known sayings is, "Information changes the seasons of your life," and I'm pleased to commend Cheryl Holland for her contribution through this book to help thousands benefit from life changing information. Don't miss your moment!

Stacia

Dr. Stacia Pierce

INTRODUCTION

I'm so excited that you've purchased and are actually reading my very first published book – Have Your Cake & Eat It Too. I've often been asked how I came up with this title. Well it's interesting that I would use a cake metaphor to write a book considering that I absolutely do not bake. The title actually started as one of my women's empowerment seminar topics. I've received so much positive feedback from that I decided to make it a book.

It started a few years ago when I'd heard someone use the statement "You can't have your cake and eat it too" and it stirred something in me. I'll be honest though, I'd heard it before but for some reason this time I had a little attitude about it. I thought wait a minute, if I actually take the time to bake a cake, you'd better believe I'm going to eat the thing. For me that's hard work. Now for some, baking a cake may be some type of relaxation or enjoyment, but for me…no way. That's work.

From that moment I thought about how when putting in the work and using what you have, that you can actually enjoy the results without guilt…the cake! It confirms my belief that anyone can change his or her life or circumstance if desired.

In this book I explore the wisdom of self development and some of the principles that have help me grow from a shy girl who once took a 0 grade on her book report in eleventh grade English class because she was too scared to read it in front of her classmates, to the woman I am today. Today I'm using my voice to empower women across the world to have their cake & eat it too. That's what my hope is for you. That this book will empower you to pursue your dreams and create the life that you really want.

The Power of Resuscitation

One of the things I know for sure is that before I give you the other principles that you need to start using is that I have to jar you out of the place that you are right now. You've been through so much in life and you're probably like I was at one point that you've just decided to just take each day as it comes. You feel like that's the best you can do. You're trying to make it through.

That mentality has to change if you're going to get the benefits from this book. You cannot have a lackadaisical attitude about your life and expect to have your cake and eat it too. You have so much more than you give yourself credit for. You have way more to offer than you believe to be true. Here's what I know.

- You've given of yourself to everyone else.
- You're there for everyone else.
- You've helped others go after their dreams.

- Your dreams have been put on the back burner.
- You're feeling stuck.

What happened to your dreams and desires? Why do you think the way your life is now is the way that it has to be? Who told you that lie and why do you believe it?

I want to shatter all of that nonsense and help resuscitate your life. Yes, some of you need life resuscitation. You're barely breathing. I know you put on the smile and cover the frustration with your mask…but enough is enough! It's time to exchange that mask that you're hiding behind for an oxygen mask so you can breath again.

Start right now…exhale!

It's going to be all right. You are going to get enough in this book to help begin to create the life that you really want. Not the one that happened. Not the one you settled for. But, the one you really want!

I need you first to believe that it's possible.

Now is not the time to worry about your family, your spouse, or your children because truth be told, if you aren't taking care of you, then you're probably not taking care of them as good as you think you are.

There's a scripture that commands us to "love our neighbors as our ourselves." Did you catch that? You cannot effectively love anyone else including your neighbor if you don't love yourself first.

It's like the metaphor that you may have heard before. When you fly on an airplane, the flight attendant instructs you to put your oxygen mask on first, before helping others. The immediate response is, "No way, I need to take care of my kids (husband, mother, best friend, stranger in the seat next to me). The idea clashes with our instinct.

What does it really mean? Simply put: If you don't put your mask on first, you won't be there for all those other people when they need you because you will be unconscious.

Are you going through life in an unconscious state because you're giving everyone else your oxygen? You can't give away what you need to sustain yourself. You need oxygen to survive. You need to breathe to survive.

Stop giving away what you need for yourself and make a decision to only give out of your overflow.

Our natural tendency is to do for others, because we are caring, loving, nurturing, responsible, supportive and competent people. However, just like the oxygen mask, we need to take care of ourselves so we can effectively take care of the people we love.

So what stands in the way of you caring for you? The most common barrier is the belief that you are being selfish if you do for yourself. That's a major misconception that women suffer from that keep them stuck.

Being selfish is lacking consideration for others or concern with ones own pleasure or profit. This is not what caring for oneself is. Taking care of ones self is being self-full not selfish. Be full and overflowing so you can give to others without killing yourself –physically, emotionally, and spiritually.

It's personal maintenance or restoring and maintaining physical, mental and spiritual health. Self-full is exercise, eating healthy, getting proper rest, having people in your life that don't drain you and taking a time out to just relax. Here's an even more simple way to look at it. What you do to take care of others—do that for you first.

Why is this so important? Burnout, depression, loneliness and physical ailments are just a few results that can happen if we neglect self-care and when we are giving while we're not self-full. A good analogy would be if you neglect your car over a period of time, do not change the oil, clean it, rotate the tires, maintain the belts etc., your car will not run very well, and eventually it will break down. The same goes for you. Self care is your personal maintenance

Self-full is your oxygen mask. It is an opportunity to breathe in new life. Put your mask on first! This is not selfish. This is being self-full to maintain your mind, body and soul.

It is the most valuable gift you can give yourself and the people who depend on you. Love yourself as much as you love others. Love ON yourself just as much as you love others. It's okay and it's necessary.

Promise yourself that from this point forward that you will love and care for yourself first. Aren't you worthy of the love you're trying to give everyone else?

Let me answer that for you, a resounding YES!

Power Affirmations:

- I am enough.
- I am worthy.
- I am worthy of loving me first..
- I am full of life and love.
- I am overflowing with love in my mind, body & spirit.
- I am committed to living beyond the status quo.
- I can have my cake and eat it too!
- I deserve the best.
- I deserve to be happy.
- I deserve to have peace.
- I deserve joy.

Power Practice:

Start small with 10-15 minute increments and build up to become self-full.

1. Take a relaxing bath and turn on your favorite music. Listening to your favorite music creates a mental recess and uplifts the spirit.

2. Take a walk or sit in the fresh air. A 5-10 minute walk outside enlivens the spirit, exercises the body to keep it healthy and helps recharge our batteries.

3. Eat the cake. Indulge and take the last piece of cake or make a favorite meal. Treating yourself makes you feel special.

The Main Ingredients

CHAPTER 1
The Right Ingredients

Every good cake starts with having the right ingredients. When talking about having your cake and eating it too, your cake is your desired success or your desired result. You want to make sure that when you have gone through life, and you've gone through whatever you've gone through that at the end of the day your desired success is what you have. I want to emphasize that we're talking about your desires and not what's expected of you from your parents, your spouse, your friends, or even your children. That's your filtered desire, not what you really want. It's what you think you should want or should do. In other words, what would really make you happy is filtered by concerns of hurting their feelings. Right now this is all about what you really want; especially if you've already raised your children and committed your life to taking care of others. It's time to take your life back and create it how you want it to be.

Taking your life back is a process! It takes time,

dedication and a determination to make it happen no matter what others think of you. After all this is your life, not theirs! If you are in the process of rediscovering YOU and getting your life back on track, or maybe you've never even been introduced to the real you at all, this book will help you do that.

I want you to get free from the bondage of living for other people at the destruction of your own happiness. Having access to the right ingredients, you can create anything that you want including a new life. When you don't like your life story, write a new one and start living it! Create your own recipe for life success with the ingredients that you already have.

You want to enjoy the fruit of your labor, you want to reap the benefits of your hard work and the trials and tribulations that you've gone through. At the end make sure that after all you've been through that you have the desired results that you want out of your life.

One thing that you have to realize is that when God made you He saw what He made and He said, "yes, that is good, you are good". So, just like a good cake you have to understand that you have all the right ingredients, you have access to everything you need to be successful in life because it's on the inside of you already and it's just waiting for you to bring it all together. You are good.

Here's where most people get stuck. Just like a cake, you

can have the ingredients, but if you have those ingredients in the cabinet or on the shelf and you're not doing anything with them, you still don't have a cake. You just have ingredients that independently can't get you what you want. You're not going to get that end result which is a good cake. Ingredients have to be brought together by mixing so that they can be effective in doing what they do. When you're preparing to bake a cake, you gather all of your ingredients, you blend them well and then you bake. It's a process. It's no different for you. You have the ingredients, however, you may need help identifying them if you don't know them, but once you've identified them you have to figure out how to blend these together to work for your benefit and to work for your life success. Once that's figured out, you stand on what you know and then go through the process.

Preparation

Let's talk about the ingredients that you already have access to. I need you to understand that it doesn't matter who you are or what your circumstances are, that you absolutely have access to enough to get your life moving in the direction you want. It starts with knowing that you can. It starts with knowing, believing, accepting, and then using what you have access to. If you're willing to start here with the right ingredients, you have what you need to have your cake and eat it too!

Every cake, no matter what kind it is, has main

ingredients. And every one of you has access to some main ingredients that I'm about to share with you now. Yes, there will be some people that may disagree with me on these, but guest what? These are the ones that I have noticed when I've studied successful people and the ones that have made the most impact on my life personally.

I've learned that successful people leave specific clues, even when they're not trying to. There are just certain characteristics that just seem to permeate from them. So these are the ones I'm going to share with you. Let's get ready to bake our cake.

Success Ingredients

1. Spiritual fortitude

Every good cake uses flour. Flour is the main ingredient that provides bulk (volume, form, substance) and structure to a cake. Your first main ingredient to real success and happiness is spirituality. Spirituality gives you structure. Structure causes you to position yourself for purpose. Without structure you'll never reach your full potential.

Successful people have a relationship with the God and creator of the universe. While some do not discuss their spiritual beliefs openly, most successful and wealthy people have a spiritual belief that grounds them for success. They understand that we are spirit beings having a human experience. This spiritual fortitude gives them the courage to get back up and try again after every failure and every disappointment. If you're functioning daily simply by using the resources given to you and not tapping into the source then eventually your resources tap out. Faith and belief from your source is what keeps you going and gives you structure for this human journey. So, tap into your spiritual source – God.

2. Attitude and perspective

Sugar is the second main cake ingredient that we'll use. Sugar provides the sweetness to the cake and makes it so good. The right attitude and the right perspective will do the same for your life. Your view of the world will impact the view of your life. Successful people have a positive attitude toward life. They're more optimistic then pessimistic. They see the glass half full instead of half empty. Successful people don't believe that everyone is against them or that everyone is up to something no good. Successful people look for the good in other people and are not suspicious at every turn. They don't complain much, but try to see the good in every situation.

If you're going through life with a negative attitude, it will keep you right where you are. One of the first things you have to do to create the life you want is to change your attitude. Have you ever been told you have an attitude problem? What's your perspective of the world? Your attitude will either attract good things or people to you or chase them away.

I'm reminded of when my granddaughter Adrianna was about three years old and she was hanging out with my aunt and me. Well she was just relaxing on the floor, laying on her back with her arms up resting under her head and watching television. She asked my aunt to get her some milk. My aunt poured the milk for Adrianna and then told her to come and get it. Little miss Adrianna then responds, "bring it to me". She didn't even say it with an attitude it was just a matter of fact tone. She was in princess mode. My aunt didn't take to kindly to that response from a three year old so she yells out to Adrianna in a firm tone, "you come and get it". Well, Adrianna, not shifting her position on the floor responds, "never mind I don't want it, you've got an attitude." I promise you it took everything in me not to bust out laughing. It was hilarious to me. It just goes to show, even children pick up on the attitude issues don't want to deal with people "with an attitude". Who are you repelling with your attitude? What level of success can you not get to because of your attitude? Add a little sugar to your life. Focus on having a positive attitude and a positive perspective. Do it on purpose. It will change your worldview and your life-view.

3. Power Words

Cakes need a leavener. A leavener like baking powder or baking soda is used to help the cake rise and give it a light texture. Your life leavener is your mouth. When you change your attitude and perspective, the other part to that is what you say. Your words have power. They can bring life and good things to you, or they can bring death and evil things to you. What you say matters. And what you say will actually help shift your attitude.

We were created to have power in our words so don't take it lightly. God created us in His image and He created this universe with His Words and gave us that same power to use words to cause things to happen. No other creation on this planet has been given the power to use their words to speak into existence what they want to happen. You've been given that power. Unfortunately what happens is when you don't know the power of your own words, you speak yourself right into a corner. If what you say is all about doom and gloom, on what's going wrong and what you don't have, then that is what you're going to produce in your life.

If in one breath you say that you want change in life or that you want a better life, then in the next breath you're talking about how broke you are and things will never change, guess what just happened. You have contradictory statements. They cancel each other out and you remain stuck right where you are. If you want to create a life that you enjoy, then watch what you say. Every word you speak is going to manifest in some way. Be intentional about what words you use if you want to change your life.

Speak positive words. Stop saying things like I'm

broke. Is that what you want to be, broke? I like what one of my pastors changed this statement too. She refused to say that she was broke but instead would say, "I have a temporary interruption in my cash flow". Things that are temporary don't last always. So when you have a temporary interruption in your cash flow just start speaking what you want to get. Create the intention for more cash flow. Do you need more clients to increase your cash flow? Then declare that new clients with the money to pay you what you deserve are coming your way. Change it up and say something different. Speak positive and you get positive. Speak negative and you'll get negative. You have what you say. Do things change overnight? Sometimes they do and sometimes you have to maintain your positive conversation until the change happens. Either way, it works.

4. Loving Me Time

The fourth ingredient in a cake is butter. Butter adds moisture to the cake and helps the batter become smooth and creamy so that it's rid of the bumps and lumps. Just like that cake batter, when all of the ingredients start coming together, there will be some lumps and bumps that need to be smoothed out. Taking the time for some "me time" is crucial to getting what you want. Loving me time can be accomplished in different ways but the bottom line is to get to a quiet place of meditation where you can relax, gather your thoughts, pray, and think clearly.

A time of meditation in the morning helps you organize

and bring focus to your day. Adding just 15 minutes in the morning to your schedule to meditate, could add hours of peace to your day. Successful people meditate. They meditate for spiritual uplifting, they meditate for relaxation, they meditate to bring focus to their lives or business, they meditate to generate ideas, they meditate to bring focus to ideas. Many reasons exist for meditation.

Meditation can be as simple as finding a place that's quiet when others in your household are asleep or otherwise occupied. Have a journal and pen ready. You can ask questions, wait for answers and write them down. Or you can simply just be, think, focus, or clear your mind. Think about your schedule for the day. Focus on the vision for your life. Clear your mind of stresses. Direct your day with meditation and see what a difference it makes in your life. Your days will be smooth and creamy and less lumpy and bumpy.

5. Growth Mindset

Egg in a cake is probably the most important ingredient because the egg holds all of the other ingredients together. It's the binder or the glue in the recipe. It adds moisture and richness as well, but the main purpose of the egg is to be the glue that holds all the dry ingredients together while baking and after. If you don't want to come unglued, you need a new mindset. Creating a success mindset is a necessary step to everything. It can either limit your potential or power your success. The way you think influences your self-esteem, your confidence, your creativity, your world-view and your resilience in the face of challenges.

The Bible says that the way you think is who you are or who you become. If you're going to change your life, changing your mind is a must. It's not a case of working longer or trying harder. Quite often the thoughts you think are the only thing that separate success from failure. The right mindset fires up your creativity, makes you more productive, motivates and inspires you when the world doubts you. It can literally change your results in an instant.

When I look back at what led to the biggest shifts in my life and my business, it's clear that changing my mindset completely altered my reality.

People with a fixed mindset typically get stuck in life. People with a growth mindset are more successful, wealthy, and happy.

World-renowned psychologist Carol Dweck of Stanford University says this about mindset and I tend to agree:

"In a fixed mindset students believe their basic abilities, their intelligence, their talents, are just fixed traits. They have a certain amount and that's that, and then their goal becomes to look smart all the time and never look dumb. In a growth mindset students understand that their talents and abilities can be developed through effort, good teaching and persistence.

They don't necessarily think everyone's the same or anyone can be Einstein, but they believe everyone can get smarter if they work at it."

When you have the mindset that you just can't do any better, then you don't do any better. Much of your success hinges on whether you believe that your abilities can be developed versus believing that they are fixed. Confidence is just displayed ability. To put it another way: Prove it to yourself in small ways and you'll develop the confidence that you can improve. Small wins repeated over time lead to a growth mindset. You can start with a small step and win today.

If you're going to be successful, you have to get your mind right! I firmly believe you can do anything that you put your mind to. Saying you're just not good at something is simply a cop-out. For example, if you say, "I'm not a math person" then that belief acts as an easy excuse to avoid practicing math. The fixed mindset prevents you from failing in the short-run, but in the long-run it hinders your ability to learn, grow, and develop new skills.

Meanwhile, someone with a growth mindset would be willing to try math problems even if they failed at first. They see failure and setbacks as an indication that they should continue developing their skills rather than a signal that indicates, "This is something I'm not good at."

Power Affirmations:

- I am a success because I have spiritual fortitude.

- My positive attitude about life brings peace to my life daily.

- The words I speak are powerful and help me create the life I want.

- I have a growth mindset that shifts me into success instantly.

Power Practice:
1. Expand and increase your reading. New information helps to stimulate and activate your success.

2. Read books and magazines that relate to self-development and help improve the way you think. A few classics to start with are:

    - As a Man Thinketh by James Allen
    - Think and Grow Rich by Napoleon Hill

CHAPTER 2
Knowing What You Want

If you are going to get what you want in life and business, guess what? You have to know what you want. You have to know your true desires. I've encountered so many women along the way who have no idea what they really want. How can you get what you want when you don't know what it is? If it shows up, how will you know that this is it?

The only way to know is to have a vision ahead of time of exactly what you want your life to be. What do you want it to look like and what is it supposed to feel like when you reach the place you've visualized.

Visualizing what you want is a major part of the process to success. So many times when people have had hard times in life they find it hard to visualize life any differently, but your imagination is on the path to getting what you want.

I know when I first started on my journey I thought the whole idea of having a "vision board" was absolutely silly.

I didn't see the point. Later I soon learned how powerful vision is.

The Bible says that people without a vision die. This is why there are so many walking dead. There is no vision. It's unconscious living with no vision for the future. The walking dead take each day as it comes. The Bible tells us to write the vision down so that when we see it we can take action.

I love this biblical example of how powerful it is to put a vision before your eyes and how that impacts the results you will see. It's the story of Jacob and his father-in-law Laban and the deal Jacob made with him that made Jacob wealthy.

Jacob offered to continue working as a keeper of the flocks if he could get the damaged animals. These were the ones that were speckled and spotted. Jacob examined the flock, removed all the speckled and spotted animals, and these were set aside as Laban's property. These animals would be taken three days' distance and kept by Laban's sons. The deal was that only those newly born spotted or striped animals would become Jacob's property. At some later time the herd would be examined, and the spotted or striped animals would go to Jacob, while the rest would be Laban's.

Removing the spotted and striped, which were in the flock, benefited Laban in two ways. First, it left these animals to him, not Jacob. Also, it lessened the chances of other spotted or striped animals being conceived, since these would not be mating with the flock and so it looked like Laban was getting the better end of the stick. It was too good to be true, Laban must have thought. How could he possibly lose?

However, it was an open-ended agreement, which encouraged Jacob to attempt to manipulate the outcome and also left God free to overrule the normal course of nature in order to bless Jacob. So what Jacob decided to do was to take fresh rods of poplar, almond and plane trees, and peeled white stripes in them, exposing the white that was in the rods. And he set the rods which he had peeled in front of the flocks in the gutters, even in the watering pots, where the flocks came to drink and mate. He kept the vision of stripes and spots in the vision of the flock.

What do you think happened? The non-stripped and non-spotted flock began producing what they saw not what they were!

That's exactly what will happen to you when you put a vision in front of your eyes daily. You will begin to produce what you see, not who you are now or what you're experiencing now! It takes your current circumstances out of the equation and your imagination eventually becomes your reality. How powerful is that?

Visual Oxygen

You must have a vision of success. You must be clear on what your desires are. What does it look like to you? Because when we use the word success it means different things to different people. My question to you is; have you really ever taken the time to think about what you really want out of life? Have you taken the time to think about it? What do you really truly want out of life? Not what's going on in your life, not what you've become accustom to, but what do you really want?

We get so busy living our day to day or going from problem to problem or crisis to crisis, that we don't take the time to really grasp or let alone plan for what we really want out of life. I believe we all have the power to create the life we desire. It's up to us to first get a picture of what success is and then we can go after it, but you have to know what success looks like to you. What is your vision of success?

Right now what I want you to do is just take a couple moments and close your eyes. Go ahead; just close your eyes for a moment. Now I want you to picture yourself in an ultimate state of success. Remove the filter of your everyday life and think about what you really want if it were possible.

- What does it look like?
- What does it feel like?
- What do you look like and what do you feel like?
- What are you doing?
- Are you working in a job or a career?

- Are you an entrepreneur calling your own shots?
- Are you an author?
- Do you have a family?
- What does your home look like?
- What does your office look like?
- What are you wearing?
- Are you traveling?

Now open your eyes. What are you doing and what does your day look like? That's how you begin to get a picture of what success looks like to you. Whatever comes to your imagination, at that very moment, is what you really want in your life or business.

If you really participated in that moment and started to picture what you really want, that is the beginning of creating a vision for your life. For some of you, that exercise was pretty hard to do because you are so involved with what your day looks like now that you can't even imagine anything different. You have so many limiting beliefs that you can't see beyond your today. But here's the thing, if you never allow your mind to imagine and visualize the future that you really truly desire you're not going to get there. You won't get there. You have to allow your mind to go there first. When your mind goes there and you begin to accept that future as a real possibility, that's when you begin to change your life. You have to have that picture in your mind. How do you know if you've reached success if you don't know what it looks like for you? Your mind has to first accept that desired state of success before your life will follow. You have to believe that the picture that you are seeing in your mind's eye is really possible for you, and it is.

You have to put vision to your vision. When you do that, it will give you focus to live out your life and to create the life you're seeing in your mind. There is a scriptural proverb that says "as a man thinks in his heart, so is he". That goes along with what you're seeing, what you think about yourself, what you think about your future, what you think about your life. When you can take those thoughts and focus them on your future and focus them on success…that is vision. That's vision and that's something very specific that you can work toward.

This is what will happen. If you know where you're going and have set intentions in that direction, then you won't be easily sidetracked by life's circumstances because you now have a focus. When you don't have something else to look at, your circumstances and your problems are what you focus on. And what you focus on expands. Your problems become bigger than they really are. Your sickness becomes worse than what it really is. Your financial lack because more oppressive than it really is.

A Vision Wall
A vision gives you something else to focus on. It gives you a focus toward your future and what you really want. You want

to be purposeful about your future. You want to frame your focus. I have two ways that I frame my focus and change my thoughts to my future. The first way is I have a vision wall. I have a vision wall that's in my office right above my desk. On this vision wall I have all sorts of images and all types of words that speak to the vision I have for my future. This particular vision wall that's right above my desk, is one that is specifically for my business. That's why I have it in my office, because it's something that I can look at while I'm sitting at my desk, especially on those days when I'm frustrated or I'm just not feeling like doing the work. My vision wall pumps life back into me because I see my future and not my feeling. I'm reminded of what I'm working so hard for. I'm reminded of what things look like on the other side of my frustration. My vision wall gives me focus and renews the hope in my dreams.

We all have days when we just don't feel like it. Simply that. No need in faking the funk like we always have it together because nobody does. But here's the thing; you need a way to jolt yourself back to where you should be which is focused on success and your future. I have that wall there to do that for me so I as I look up I can see those things that are part of my future, that vision that I'm working toward and that motivates me. It keeps me going. It keeps me focused. I know I'm working toward a specific end, a purposed end. I don't allow my current situation or whatever I may be going through on a particular day to distract me for long or to cause me to slow down, to look back or want to turn around because I have a vision right before me. That's what I'm working toward. That is my focus.

Vision Manifesto

My other visual oxygen is what I call my "vision manifesto". It's actually a portfolio book that I used to use for my graphic design samples. I have it in sections. It is a little different than my vision wall. My vision wall has different types of pictures and words just for my business. My vision manifesto is the vision for every area of my life. It's much more organized and it's portable. In other words, if I'm traveling or if I just want to sit on my bed and look at it, then I have it right in front of me. It's not this huge board that can only be stationary in my home. I can carry my vision around with me. It's in a binder with protective sheet covers, and I have organized it into three sections. This is what I did for me. You can organize yours, if you desire to create one, in whatever type sections that work best for you. Mine has three sections. It has my spiritual life, it has my business life, and it has my home life. For each of those, I have pictures and I have words that resonate with me and help me to visualize my future and to keep me on track. I look at that constantly to remind me of what I'm working toward. I also look at it to keep it fresh in my mind, because as you to look at it, it becomes more and more real.

As you work toward your vision, you can feel it getting closer and closer. It becomes more of you. It becomes more of your life. Even if it's not the physical life right now, in your mind's eye and in your mind that is your life. You are attracting that life to you by focusing on it, because what you focus on expands. You either have to focus on your vision for your future or you are going to focus on your current circumstances that you obviously don't like. You're not satisfied with where you are and you're not satisfied with the status quo so what do you want to focus on? Do you want to focus on a vision for the future? Or, do you want to focus on what you are going through right now? Whatever you spend your time focusing on, that is what will expand and dominate your life. If you desire to do a vision wall or vision book, I think it's a wonderful tool that you can have, that you can touch, that you can see, that you can grab a hold of to keep you focused on your vision. These are just your vision points of contact. They should answer the questions "Where am I going? What does my future look like?" You have to be able to answer those questions before you actually get there. If you don't know where you're going, how do you know you've gotten there? How do you create the life you want if you don't know what you want?

Enlarge Your Vision

The other part that I want to share with you is don't be afraid to think big. We have to get beyond only thinking what we can see as possible with our natural eye. If you have a vision and it doesn't scare you just a little bit or it doesn't make you a little bit nervous to say it out loud, then it's not big enough. You have to think and do something big to cause a shift in your life.

I want you to think big, but I don't want you to get paralyzed by bigger. Just because you can't see how it's going to happen, doesn't mean that it won't happen. See it by faith. As you see it by faith, you will begin to get the strategies on how you can get there. You have to think big and continue to allow room for more than what you can even ask or think. Think big! Know what success looks like to you! Write it down! Put it in pictures! It's your future? Frame it and focus it! As long as you focus on your purpose, you'll be able to create a vision and the goals to help you get there.

Power Affirmation:
- I deserve to have what I see in my vision.
- Everything I see in my future IS possible.
- My future is successful.
- My vision resuscitates the power in my life to get what I want.

Power Practice:
1. If you do not have a vision board, wall or manifesto, get started today creating your vision.
2. Don't be afraid to visualize BIG.
3. Place your vision in a location that you must see it

every single day.

4. Write up to three small goals toward your vision daily and do them.

CHAPTER 3
Doing It With Intention

Desires lead to attention, which can also be called an intention. Intention gives you a push to get all the energy that goes into getting what you want.

A recent study found that 87% of people spend more time planning their vacations than they do planning their lives, finances, relationships and other aspects of their life. So it really comes as no surprise that people have more success pulling off a vacation than they do improving their lives - they simply take the time to plan their vacation.

Why does planning lead to results? Because when you plan something your intention is clear! You want to go on a vacation and you want to enjoy it so you focus on the rewards of being on vacation and you begin doing exactly what you need to do in order to complete and enjoy your vacation. It starts as a desire and then you set your intention to make it happen.

Now what if you used this same process in every aspect of your life?

I call it the Power Of Intention and when you begin to utilize the Power Of Intention - you will begin to get dramatic results in your life. When you have the Power Of Intention working for you, you'll begin moving in the direction of achieving your goals and creating the life you really want.

Now, don't get it twisted, good intentions and the Power Of Intention are two very different things.

Good intentions are a dime a dozen because it doesn't require any action. Anyone can say they have good intentions but that does not mean that you're going to be purposeful about it. The Power of Intention is, well, intentional.

The Bible gives a good example of the power of intention when it says to focus your thoughts on whatever is true, whatever is honorable, whatever is just, whatever is pure, whatever is lovely, or whatever is commendable. This is one of the things you would do instead of worrying about your troubles or issues. Change your intention. Change your focus to what is good and what you want to see. What you see in your vision's eye, not what you see before you at any given moment.

A Different View

If you want to begin to change something in your life, you

have to first change the way you look at it. See a bad life situation as an opportunity to shift, to move in a direction of your new desire. You can use every bad situation and everything that happens in your life that you do not want as a seed to grow what you do want.

Once you see something that you do not like, begin to search for an intention, declare a path and then start taking action in that direction. It's not good enough to just know what you desire, you actually have to do some work in the direction of your goal.

The reason why we sometimes manifest what we want and sometimes we don't is because we are not always sending forth our intent. Sometimes we consciously intend for something to manifest and therefore we experience it happening. But then at other times we forget to consciously intend it and then it does not manifest during those times. Everything happens by intent and we have to keep choosing in every moment what we want to experience. You have to intend what you want again each time.

Be on Purpose
Do things on purpose and don't be afraid to let your motives show when you do something to get what you want. You deserve it. Period. When you hold back it's just proof that you have limiting beliefs about what you can achieve. Or, you're worried about what others think. You have to get to a place where you don't care what other people think. Their

opinion about your future doesn't mean a thing. Others have no claim in your future except what you want to give them. You can have whatever you want and let others know it.

It is the nature of everyone to do things with intention because God created the whole universe to operate by intention. He set the intention for light to exist and it came to be, he set intention for the sun to be positioned where it is, and there it stays. And He set the intention for you to have creative power when He created you in His image. When you allow yourself to act according to your intentions and do things on purpose, you will find yourself getting more and more of what exactly it is you want.

Example of Intention in Dating
The Power of Intention should be used in any given situation. When you go to a place to be with attractive members of the opposite sex, go there with your intention in mind. Don't go there pretending to yourself that you are just there just to have fun when your true desire is to meet someone that you're attracted to. You want to meet someone who could potentially be a husband. Yes, you want to have fun and not be too intense with your intention but don't fake like you don't want to meet someone special.

Too many women act like they can't let their intentions be known relating to wanting a husband because they are "waiting on God" or "they're waiting on their Boaz". I'm just going to be real transparent right here—that burns my tail! First off, nowhere in the Bible does it say that God is a matchmaker. He didn't arrange marriages, people did. Not only that, if you're going to use Ruth and Boaz as an example, Ruth positioned herself so Boaz could see her. She was in position and then he "found" her. He wasn't out looking for her. Many like to quote the scripture that says when a man "finds" a wife, he finds a good thing as if a man is going to knock on your door and say, hey you're the one I've been looking for. It doesn't work that way. Don't be afraid to position yourself to be found. He still has to seek after you to make you his wife, but there's nothing wrong with having your intentions known. Now, if you want to stay single then keep listening to the advice from married folk who have a warm body at night. Position, but don't pursue. Okay, that's all for that because this topic wasn't my intent for this book but wanted to make sure I said my peace on that issue. Here's the thing. When you don't focus your intention, you put a half-hearted energy into your intent and create half way results. You may be there to have fun as a way of detaching from your intention, but you still keep your primary focus in mind and not lose track of what you want.

Example of Intention in Getting Wealthy

When you want to become wealthy, you must do everything with the intention of becoming wealthy. You must intend to be wealthy, not just having enough or having a lot. Rich means rich! That is exactly what you intend and you do not intend anything else. That is why only the few get rich and the rest of the people do not. The rich have gotten where they are because they did everything with the intention of becoming rich and nothing less than that. When you intend to be rich, the power to create wealth activates inside of you. I've learned that wealthy people don't love money; they love the freedom that money provides.

Don't be afraid of having money and lots of it at that. It's okay. Money isn't evil; the Bible says it's the love of money that's the problem. The same Bible also says that money answers all things and it does. You can help more people if you have more money. For most of you money would solve just about any problem you have going on right now. Open yourself up to have more of it.

Don't block your wealth blessing because you're afraid to want money or afraid to let anyone know that you want more money. There's not a thing wrong with it.

Focus and Shift

With busy schedules and to-do lists that carry us from hour to hour without much time to breathe, it's rare that we stop to think about our motivations. But when we take the briefest of moments to set clear, positive intentions for what we're doing, the payback is huge. We can make a shift in how any assignment, conversation, or meeting feels just by focusing on where we want to place our attention.

Our perception of the world is much more one-sided

than we tend to realize because our brains have limited processing power. If we tried to pay attention to every tiny object, sound, and sensation, we'd freeze like an overloaded computer. So we subconsciously prioritize information that seems most related, with related meaning simply as whatever we choose to place at the top of our minds. The result is that we'll focus on whatever connects with our mood, our expectations, our concerns, and then we filter out the rest.

That filter is pretty personal and naturally it means we sometimes miss important parts of the story; even our own story. Research shows that we have what's called an "inattentional blindness". If we're not paying attention to it then basically we don't really see it. We may even twist information so that it more neatly fits our expectations. This is how you can dislike someone that you don't even know simply based on what someone told you. You've already created an expectation in your mind, so when you meet them you may see what you "expect" to see.

At work, this means we may fail to perceive the good things a colleague does if we've already formed a belief that they're annoying. And if we're in a bad mood starting a task, we can easily end up paying attention to problems more than solutions. We rarely realize it, because we don't know what we don't notice. When we rush through our days without reflection, our mental filters are on this kind of automatic setting.

But it's possible to be more deliberate in choosing what deserves our attention. Because if we consciously decide what's really most important to us — on this day, in this interaction, during this task — we can be more proactive and intentional with what we notice and remember. We can take off our blinders and see more of the reality we want to see. In short, we can change our experiences.

If you have an attitude with everyone you meet or have difficulty with every job you work on, I have news for you. It's not them; it's you. Your filter is off which means your expectations are most likely off too and an attitude adjustment is definitely in order. Are you ready to change your experiences?

Power Affirmations:
- My success is intentional.
- I have the power to create a new experience.
- I purposely shift to the good in every situation.

Power Practice:
1. Check in with yourself. Ask yourself what's at the top of your mind right now. What are your expectations, about the situation and the people you're dealing with? What needs or concerns do you have? What's your mood?

2. Decide on a positive intention. Identify what matters most to you. If you're coming up with anything negative, reframe it to a positive.

CHAPTER 4

Put a Demand on Your Potential

You have what it takes. No matter what talents you were born with, what family you were born into, the money you have made or lost, the times of difficulty or what you may consider as lucky breaks, nothing will get you to where you want to be better than understanding your full potential.

It's the common theme in every success story—the people who succeed are the people who learn how to tap into something inside of them to live and breathe their dreams. That's the key...it's already inside of you!

You have a hidden treasure in you! That treasure is called potential. You have absolute potential inside of you. The brilliant part is that you have a potential that is uniquely yours. It's a mix of your genetics, your environment, the way your body has been designed and the talents you were born with. You have something different. You have a God-given gift that you can share with world. That gift is one of the things that make you authentic. It's also one of the things that will propel you to prosperity if you will take the time to uncover it, and then invest in it. Yes, invest. When you spend time and or money on your personal growth, it's a worthy investment.

The first step, of course, is discovering exactly what that gift is so that you can maximize your potential. For some people this is may be a natural process, most likely because they were helped by a watchful parent or teacher that saw something in them from an early age and called it into being. How did they call it into being? By encouraging them to pursue their interests, by telling them they were great even when their behavior said otherwise, and by continually supporting opportunities for their growth. But unfortunately what is more common, I think based on my own experiences and people who I've coached, is that we really don't discover the power of our potential until well into adulthood after we have gathered life experiences of our own that we have learned from. However, none of that destroys the potential that you have. You still have it. It may be dormant and starving for some attention, but it's in there.

For many people it's a struggle to identify their potential. That can be for a whole lot of reasons. We often have an instinct or inkling of what we want to do as young children. But this can be torn from us by expectations that don't match our own natural talents or pushed down by our parent's or family disapproval. So, since it's been pushed down it now needs to be pulled out. For instance you may be a creative person who loves to put colors and designs together, but you were told that you should be an accountant, teacher or even a blue collar worker. There may be an expectation that you'll be working in that same field all of your adult life. Or maybe you've come from an environment where there were drugs, crime and social services as a way of life. So you've been told all of your life that you aren't worth anything and never will be. It doesn't matter what the scenario, the end scenario is the same. You're not living to your fullest potential.

Environment plays a major role

We often learn about what we are good at through trying new things. If you were raised in an environment where there weren't a lot of options, or you didn't have a lot of money to pay for classes or for travel, then you may not have experienced the things you that are naturally good at.

Sometimes our lack of ambition, mixed with limiting false beliefs can get in the way. We'll use our creative person as an example. She is a talented and creative designer who loves to put concepts together. However she was raised in a poor family and had experienced that embarrassing feeling of frequently being the only kid in her class without the cool shoes, trendy fashions or the latest gadget. While she loved design, she felt it couldn't make her money so she went for the more traditional methods such as finance and accounting. No matter how hard she stuck with it she found herself stressed, unhappy and even worse, poor because she couldn't seem to climb up the ladder to success. She was starving her passion and potential. Is that you?

Finally in desperation she starts to do some designing for friends on the side just to keep her sane. At first it was a free thing, but as her designs were shown to others, people started to ask to pay her. She discovered that you could actually be doing something you loved AND get paid for it. She just wishes that she'd known a lot earlier. Imagine how much further along she'd be.

Our potential can also be cut short by circumstance. If you are struggling to meet bills every week, and you have a family to support or other responsibilities, it can be hard to see your way out of it to unlock that missing key and find success in the things you were born to do.

Whatever the reason or reasons that have brought you to want to unlock your potential, the most important thing from here on in is that none of that has to matter. For every time you've struggled and stressed that you'll never find your passion and then be able to use it, there is a person who has learned how to do that very thing. And guess what? If they can do it, well you can too.

What's In Your Bag?
What do you have inside of you that is your bag of gold? What's that thing that could turn everything around for you and take you to your wealthy place? When we talked

about the main ingredients, this could actually be a sixth one. Flavoring. What is your flavor?

Do you know that it's your responsibility to be profitable? God works with increase! And the key to see the increase in every area of your life is tied to what's in your bag? You have a bag of gold! I don't know how much gold is in your bag but you have at a minimum one piece of gold in your bag that can change your life.

God has invested a part of himself in you. There's a unique part of God that he's put in you that makes you unique. When He created you in His image, He made an investment in you! He made an investment and He wants a return. It's irresponsible to have missed opportunities to use your gifts and talents to bring in wealth. They are a conduit for wealth and blessing in your life. Most of your financial struggles would be over if you focused without fear on using your gifts and invest in the information needed to get specific strategies to implement them and bring you profit.

A great example
The parable of the talents is a great example of the disappointment in those who allow fear to cause them to shrink back and not use what you have to bring increase to your life. In Biblical times "talent" meant something very different than when we think of talent today. The talents in the parable were talking about a whole lot of money. A talent was a gold coin and it was actually the largest unit

of money at the time. Someone who had five talents of gold or silver was a multimillionaire by today's standards. Some calculate the talent in the parables to be the same as 20 years of wages for the common worker. Needless to say (but I'll say it anyway), knowing the actual meaning, weight, and value of a term like talent can help give deeper understanding and better perspective.

If the talents were gold, the value of what was entrusted to the stewards would be extremely high, in the millions of dollars. It seems reasonable to assume that the owner of the talents, the man traveling into a far country, was a wealthy man. He is entrusting his wealth to three men who become stewards of his money. One receives five talents. Another receives two talents. A third steward receives one talent. Each is given a lot of money. Can you imagine someone saying to you, "here take care of a few million for me until I get back?" What?

So these are stewards responsible with the care of a big sum of money. The amount given is based on each steward's ability. The first two understand the spirit and letter of instructions given to them. They both use the resources by "trading" to gain a profit. Each of them makes a 100 percent profit. But fear and mistrust motivate the third steward. He buries the money and returns the original amount. The profitable stewards are praised, given increased responsibilities. The distrusting steward is scolded, rejected, and punished.

Wow! Which side of this equation do you want to be on? What's that talent or gift in you that could be making an increase in your life?

Start Studying

You need to study yourself to discover what your difference is. What makes you uniquely you? What do you love to do? What do people around you come to you for? What do you seem to be naturally good at?

What do others tell you that you're good at? What do you do that causes you to loose track of time because you're so engaged in it? That difference holds the key to your future! Your gift, and talent, is used as your brand, to bring in wealth and increase.

Mike Murdock says, "Your similarity creates your comfort, but your difference creates your rewards." If you don't know your difference or uniqueness, you become a hostage to what other people want you to be.

Unfortunately for me, I didn't really begin to study myself and ask myself these questions until after I went through a divorce. I was asking questions about myself that I could not answer. Imagine that! You're asking questions about yourself, and you can't answer them. We sometimes get so lost in our day-to-day life, trying to please others and living up to other's expectations that we lose focus of who we really are.

God has placed a part of Himself in you that nobody else has. It's the part of Him, especially for you. What is that? Take the time to find out what He's invested in you because what makes you different is the same thing that makes you important, valuable, and relevant. It's your bag of gold!

Commit

Eventually you have to move from good intentions to commitment. Good intentions don't cause increase. Get to a place where you translate your intention into actual results.

- You have to commit to being successful
- You have to commit to your dreams
- You have to commit to causing a shift in your life

You know the saying, "the more things change, the more things stay the same." Life is changing, the world is changing all around you but if you don't change life will have passed you by and you'll not have accomplished all that you could have. Do you really want to be at the end of this life with the regrets of could haves, should haves, and I was going to?

You have to start somewhere, and that somewhere is right where you are now. Commit to taking some kind of action that is in alignment with your intention. You already know enough, you are already qualified enough, and yes you are enough! Start with being crystal clear on what you want, how much you want and when you want it.

Take the Plunge

More than anything I want you to start your pursuit today. Pursue your dreams and pursue your passions. Pursue that business you want to start, pursue that ministry that's been in your spirit, and pursue your passions.

It's time to take the plunge and block out the naysayers or so-called haters. They can't see your dream and they aren't supposed to…it's yours!

Imagine you're on an island. It's just you, God, the island and you're surrounded by ice-cold water. You've been praying to God saying, "get me off of this island." Now, out in the distance you see a boat. But you have to get to that boat. If you want to survive and get off of that island, your only option is to jump in that cold water and start swimming to that boat. So you're standing there looking down at that icy cold water…you are afraid to dive into that water, but you know you need to take that plunge to get to your boat. So how do you do it?

- Do you go in one toe at a time?
- Do you stand there for a while waiting for just the right moment?
- Do you stand there and pray for God to drop an

angel on the island to give you a push?
- Do you keep praying and asking God to get you off the island when you have a boat right in front you?

No. You have to just do it. Just dive in! Take the plunge. You've done all the thinking and praying you need to do. Just dive in! Once you dive in, yes it will be freezing cold, but you're in and on your way and the movement will warm you up. Now you have no choice but to keep on swimming to the boat. And guess what? As you get closer to the boat, someone on that boat will see you and come to meet you to carry you the rest of the way.

That's how it is with your dreams. You can't wait for the right moment to come along, or for someone to give you a push or for the water to heat up to just the right temperature. Just dive in!

You have to take the plunge. Pursue. Pursue. Pursue. Pursue like that man you've been pursuing and he's not even the one anyway. How do I know? Because you're pursuing him instead of him pursuing you. I'm just saying, shift your energy! Put a demand on your potential and activate your difference so that you can change your life. It's time out for sitting on the sidelines of your own life. Take center stage and own it!

You are sitting on a gold mine, and have a bag of gold in your hand. What are you going to do with it?

Power Affirmations:
- I have access to everything I need to change my life already inside of me.
- My gifts, talents, and my difference make me wealthy.
- I am committed to pursue my dreams.

Power Practice:

To activate the power of your potential you have to make some lifestyle changes:

1. Replace your comfort zone with a confidence zone – get comfortable being uncomfortable. If you're comfortable, then you're in the wrong spot. You should always feel challenged. If you're not being challenged you're not producing an increase.

2. Make connections with people and information. Somebody has the information you need to get you where you need to be. I'm talking about the specific action steps that you have to take. The right people and the right information will change your life.

CHAPTER 5

Stay in the Oven

Have you been working and working but the results just don't seem to be there? You want what you want, and you're ready for it now. There's nothing wrong with that and because of your persistence you will get there. But here's the thing, getting to the place in life where you really want to be is a process! There is no getting around it. It's part of life and it makes you who you are so that you can handle the success when you get there. Never despise the process. It can be painful but it will all work for you in the end. Trust the process even when things heat up!

I know that many of the things I went through including my divorce and everything that happened after that has been part of my process. Lord knows I could've given up during that time because it was so difficult. However, because of my faith and my tenacity to get to my promise and the vision I had for my life, I could not give up in the process. I decided to take the heat and stay in the oven.

The key is to trust the process and endure the necessary parts of the path. Use this time as an opportunity get stronger spiritually, refocus your purpose, and get clarity on your next steps.

I like the Bible reference of Abram as a great example of going through a process. It says that it was by faith Abraham, when called to go to a place he would later receive as his inheritance, that he obeyed and went, even though he did not know where he was going.

He was told to go to a place that later he would receive as an inheritance. In other words, God had a promise for him but said to Abram; you're not going to get that until later! There is a process before the promise. The promise is later but the process is now. Profiting from passion is later but the process is now. Living in your purpose is later, but the process is now.

The story goes a little something like this. Abram was told to get away from his kinfolk and go to a place that God had shown him. But he was stuck in a place called Haran until his father died. Haran means "parched" or dried up. He was on the journey to the Promised Land with his father and other family members but got stuck! Is this what's holding you up? You're on your way to the promise but you're stuck because there are people on the journey with you who were not given that same Promised Land vision?

Abram stayed in Haran until after his father died. After that he left Haran with his nephew and went to the place of Canaan and there was famine in the land when he got there. Although he reached the place, he had not reached the promise of Canaan. Canaan is known as the place that flows with milk and honey. It was a wealthy place. But when Abraham arrived, there was a famine in the land. So Abram could get to the place with his nephew, but he couldn't get to the promise! Remember, God had told him to leave all of his family, not some but all.

Don't Delay Your Promise

You have to stop attaching yourself to people that are not part of your promise because they are delaying and lengthening your process to get there! Even if they are family, if they're not part of your promise, then they simply cannot go. Be careful not to sabotage your own success worrying about others. As adults we are responsible for ourselves. Your adult children and other family members are not your responsibility. Are you really willing to forfeit your promise and success for those who really should be focusing on their own journey?

Trying to pull family into the promise is not the only way you can delay your promise. Attaching yourself to a person who isn't part of the promise can happen in many ways. Being jealous of what somebody else has or what he or she is doing will keep from your promise as well. You could have your own promise if you'd just get yourself and other folk out of the way. Holding on to hate and disdain for people that you should've forgiven a long time ago. Holding on to relationships that should've been cut off a long time ago. And I'm going to throw this in for good measure. Ladies, please stop looking for a man to take care of you. Be that Proverbs 31 woman. She had her stuff together. She handled business and had her own. Her husband bragged on her because of it and her children called her blessed. Two people in alignment and being processed toward a promise; now that is powerful. There's a process to the promise!

Let me get back to Abram. Movement brings clarity. God gave Abram a glimpse of the vision but He doesn't add clarity to the vision until after Abram separated from his nephew. After the nephew left, God told Abram to look as far as his eyes could see. All of the land was his. God told him to leave his family and go where he was instructed. Be ready to move at a moments notice. When you get an idea that will get you closer to what you really want, don't hesitate but take fast action toward that destination. Move!

Make room for more

Giving is part of the process. As you give of your time, money and resources you open up room to receive more. Trying to hold on to the old things that you have, leaves little room for the new that you're expecting. A principle that all successful people abide by is giving. You cannot receive more if you're stingy. A closed hand doesn't give, but it also can't receive either.

If you're feeling stuck, perhaps it's because you're out of alignment with the path you should be on for your journey. Or maybe some people on the path with you need to be removed.

Everything you've seen as the vision of your life isn't going to happen if you don't work your way through the process. There is a process to the promise. That person you're trying so hard to take along with you hasn't been prepared for your journey, you have. Cut the string! That's your promised land, that's the place promised to you based on your struggles, your tears, your pain, and your processing. They have to go through their own process to get their promised land. My promised land doesn't look exactly like your promised land so your process can't be used to get me to my promise! You have to walk this thing out yourself!

Power Affirmations:
- I trust the process to my promise.
- I give of myself, my time and my finances so that I have room for more.
- I let go over every person and every thing that is hindering my progress to my promise.

Power Practice:
1. Connect with the right process partner to keep you encouraged when the heat is on.
2. Evaluate your relationships to determine who needs to be disconnected from your process.

CHAPTER 6
Create a Curb and Kick'em There

Each of us has people or things that we value that are important to us and help make up our core. Your values are what give you value. You have value when you care enough about yourself and your wellbeing to set the boundaries. Successful people who get what they want in life and business have clear boundaries in all areas of their lives.

Your values help you set the boundaries in your life so that you don't allow others to come into to your private space, your success, and your vision for your life to wreck havoc over what you've worked so hard for.

Boundaries are meant to be clear and known. Here's the thing. Your boundaries teach people how to treat you. Every relationship in your life should have boundaries. Some will have generous boundaries that give those who you hold most valuable broader access to you. Others will have a very limited boundary.

When you're headed for success and working toward creating the life you want, your circle will get smaller and smaller and you have to be okay with that. For you to reach the success you desire you have to build associations around the purposes and plans for your life. Do not underestimate the influence that other people have in increasing or decreasing your value. It is your responsibility to be aware of your circle and what they are influencing.

The people that you should allow in your environment should have no problem respecting your boundaries. And, that's your clue that let's you know if they should be there. When you have preset boundaries, it makes it easier to say no to those things that don't align with your purpose and desires for your life.

I have a very small circle of friends that I keep in my life. The people who have access to my inner circle are only those who have proved themselves worthy. I know where I'm headed and the vision for my life so I don't take my associations lightly and neither should you.

You've heard the saying, "birds of a feather flock together". Well, it may not be absolutely true but perception is reality. Especially when you're working toward a successful lifestyle focused on getting what you want. Stick with the people that have similar values as you. Here's the thing you have to realize. Those who are in your inner circle, who you are afraid of letting go maybe because you don't want to hurt their feelings, are the very ones who will turn their backs on you when your success starts hitting them in the face. Why? Your success will shine the light on what they have not accomplished. You having the audacity to go after your dreams and the nerve to actually reach them will be offensive to those who haven't done the same. Their insecurity will show up in jealousy and negativity.

Get rid of the dead weight.
There are some things in your life and some people in your life that are just dead weight. They don't bring anything to the table of your life and they're always draining you. They are not good for you and guess what, they are grown and not your responsibility. Get yourself together and then just maybe you can be of some real help to them but right now…they look better gone!

I've shared on my blog examples of friends that need to be fired and I think I need to repeat them here. You have to weed the garden of your life by choice. Who are the weeds and who are flowers? When you want more out life…more happiness, more peace, and more stability, and even more money— many times the first step toward those goals is to prune the weeds in your life to make room for the flowers. When you purpose to remove negative people, places, and things from your life you'll find more freedom and confidence in yourself, you'll put more effort into and strengthen those relationships that do matter, and you'll attract more like-minded positive people into your life. One of the best things for you to do to better your life is to cut a friendship that brings you down. Be empowered to let go and keep it moving!

Friends that look better gone!

Tammy Tolerate

That "friend" you tolerate. Why is that? Why do you have so called friends that you tolerate? You have nothing in common and your future plans don't align with hers. There has to come a time in your life when you understand who you are and what your purpose is. Not everyone is going to be a life-long friend. Some are only in your life for a specific reason or a season. When you take the friendship past its time that's not good for you or that friend. Why would you want expired things in your life? Would you eat expired food? Would you take expired medicine? Now if you answered yes to either of those then your issues may be deeper than just tolerating people who have expired in your life.

Find the courage to separate yourself from relationships that are not serving a purpose. Those types of friendships are high school. As an adult woman who has desires and intention for success in her life, you have to make the sometime hard decision to let people go. Yes, her; the one that just came to your mind while you were reading this.

Fake Fay

Fake Friend, I mean Fay always forgets to return calls for weeks and sometimes months, doesn't show up for your special occasions and most times is just missing in action until she needs something. She makes plans to meet up with you but then she's always showing up late or changing plans at the last minute because "something came up". Let's face it. In this situation, you are "Tammy Tolerate". She is not a real friend to you and is simply tolerating you for whatever reason. Don't give her the satisfaction. You're fabulous yourself and you do not have to be friend needy.

Find and spend time with those who do celebrate and appreciate you as a friend and who are interested in your life, not just tolerating you. You are better than that. Even if you were friends with this person for years, you may have just grown apart. And that's okay. It happens in all types of relationships. It's time to move on to someone who has friendship to give.

Negative Nancy

Hey, we all have our moments. That time when we're caught off-guard or something happens that just gets us in a negative place temporarily. Hopefully those moments are far and few between. On the other hand there are some people who are always negative. Something is wrong with everything and everybody. The perpetual pessimist will always have you using way too much energy to counteract all the negativity. How much energy are you using for every positive you share with her and she counters with a negative? How much energy are you using when for every negative she throws at you, you have to come up with a positive to talk yourself back up from the conversation with her? That is too draining.

Evaluate whether this is a relationship you should be in. If it's someone that you can't get rid of too easily, like family, then set boundaries around your time and conversation with them. Just because they're family does not give them the right to pour their negativity into your life. Love is still love from a distance. Respect is still respect from a distance.

Drama Debbie

Have you met someone who just seems to attract drama? No matter where she is, she seems to encounter a problem. She's always the one with hair in her food at the restaurant, she's always having someone look at her funny, she's always the one that someone was rude to, she's always the one who got the wrong order of whatever, and she's always the one that people are giving her a hard time. She is a magnet for drama! Know this, when someone is always having an issue no matter what they're doing, no matter where they go, no matter where they work…it's not the other people it's them!

So, unless you're also a Drama Debbie, you should minimize your time with this type of person. She is the common denominator in every dramatic scenario that she pulls you into and until she owns that and changes, drama will follow her and you. Do you really have time for that? If your answer is no, then what are you going to do about it? Snip, Snip! Cut her loose and keep it moving. You're on the road to success and getting what you want. You do not have time for that.

Helpless Halle
She's the friend that you always have to help with something but she can help you with nothing. It's always one sided. You've accomplished things, you're educated or in school, you're well read, you manage your money well, and you're on a road to success, yet you are holding on to Helpless Halle. There's nothing wrong with offering help and even being in the place of needing help every now and then. But what about if she is always the one needing the help but never has anything to offer to help you?

These one-sided relationships are off balance, unhealthy and do not suit the woman who wants more out of life. Maybe you were in that helpless place at one time but you decided that you wanted something different, so you did something different and are now living something different. If this person was in your life then, and you don't want to seem like you're abandoning them now that you're getting yourself together, here's some advice that may help. The next time she comes to you to borrow money or for some other help, ask her what her plan is to change her situation so that she doesn't have to keep depending on your help. It's simple. If she doesn't have a plan, don't give any more help because it's a never-ending black hole. If she does have a plan, then offer to be her accountability partner so you can help her stick to her plan and decide what, if any, help you will give for a predetermined amount of time. Pick a time frame and stick with it.

The bottom line is this, never allow yourself to get hung up on friendships that are bringing you down or hindering the progress you're trying to make in your life. Be okay with the fact that as you grow in your success that some people in your life can't come along. They have their journey and you have yours. At some point those paths may no longer cross. Always remember that the separation does not have to be bitter, but it should always make you better. Get yourself a success strut and be willing to walk away from anything or anyone that doesn't add value to your life. If your every encounter with them is filled with negativity, stress, and angst then why are they in your life? Create a curb and kick them there.

Power Affirmations:
- I value my life.
- My circle of influence is small and only includes people proven worthy.
- I let go of everyone who does not add value to my life.

Power Practice:

1. Write down boundaries for every area of your life: spiritual, physical, and emotial.
2. Create an inner boudary and an outer boundary for each area.
3. Evaluate your relationships to determine who belongs in what boundary.

CHAPTER 7
Get out of Your Own Way

What if I told you that most of what you're dealing with that is blocking your success and keeping you from getting what you want in life is you? The only one that's stopping you is you. It's time to get out of your own way so you can create the life and business you really want.

Yes, get out of your own way. You might be asking yourself, "How am I in my own way?" Let's start with all of the excuses that you come up with to convince yourself why you can't accomplish something.

- Why you can't be successful.
- Why you can't follow your dreams.
- Why you can't write that book.
- Why you can't start the business that you desire.

These are all excuses. We have to learn how to get out of our own way. You have all of the right ingredients to be successful, but you have to be determined to do something with them. I promise you that no matter what excuse you come up with, it doesn't matter what it is… the I don't have the money excuse, I'm a single parent excuse, I don't have the time lie, or the I'm too old to do anything excuse. The excuses you come up with are endless. It doesn't matter what the excuse is. For every excuse that you can come up with, I'm sure I can find somebody who was in a very similar situation and decided not to use excuses, but they instead decided to do something to make a change in their own lives.

One of the powerful stories of someone, who had very legitimate reasons not to go after his dreams or think that he could be successful by the way, is that of Nick Vujicic. Nick was born with no arms and no legs yet he travels around the world telling others that they are enough. He wants others to know that it's a lie to think that you're not worth anything. He encourages those that he comes in contact with to achieve whatever they want in their lives; that if he could do it with no arms or no legs, then so can they. He played the hand he was dealt and is winning.

As a young man, Nick was bullied and harassed in school and even attempted suicide at the age of 10. But he had a mindset change, accepted who he was and decided to stop making excuses and to change his life. He discovered the power of taking control of his own life. He refuses to let physical limitations dictate his life. So, with no arms and with no legs he golfs, snorkels, surfs and plays soccer. He's traveled to 44 countries with his message and yes; he found love and married the love of his life. So tell me, what's your excuse again? There is no legitimate one that you can come up with to convince me that you can't accomplish whatever you want to in life. Nick makes every excuse you can come up with sound absolutely silly. Look up Nick Vujicic on YouTube and I promise he will inject you with unbelievable hope for your own future.

Make a Grand Entrance

Are you ready to show up and make an entrance? Make a grand entrance into your own life story. If you don't like the way your story is going, if you don't like the way your life is going, then it's time for you to re-write your story. That's what Nick did. He changed the direction of his life. In spite of the bullying and the torture he went through because of his physical limitations, he flipped the script on his own life story. You have the power in you to do the same thing. You have the capability in you. It starts with making a decision to get out of your own way. To go for what you want in life. You have the availability to do that. You have the power to do that already on the inside of you. You have to make a decision to show up in your own life and make something happen. The only thing stopping you from being the success that you want and having what you want out of life is you. It's you and your excuses.

Stop the Blame Game

The other part to getting out of your own way is to stop hanging with your friend "Heshethey". Your friends he, she and they. These are people who you are always blaming for why you can't accomplish something. He did this. She did that. They did this. Blame. Blame. Blame. Blaming other people keeps you stuck. So, if you're stuck, you're stuck by choice or you're stuck by ignorance. When I say stuck by ignorance, I'm saying that you're stuck and you might not know how to get out of it. You don't know what to do. You may not even know that you're stuck. You might just think this is just a way of life and that this is the way it's supposed to be.

Some people are stuck by choice. You know this is not the life that you're supposed to be living. You know that there's more you should be doing. You know that there's more inside of you than what you're giving out and what people are seeing, but you've made a choice that you're just going to be stuck. Sometimes you may not know how to get out of it and sometimes you may need to have someone help you out of it, and that's okay. That's what I do as a coach is help woman get unstuck. That's understandable. But, when you know you're stuck and you don't care that you're stuck, you're stuck by choice. Why would you want to spend any more time blaming other people?

Something may have happened to you when you were a child. Many people go through traumatic experiences as children. But, many people also come out of that and use that situation to make their lives a success and help other people. It's all about how you go about it, your perspective of whether you're going to put blame on somebody else and just stay suck, or whether you're going to show up in you own life and re-write your story to make something happen. Yes, some things that happened to you as a child you had no control over, but as an adult you have absolute control. You can choose not to let that dictate the rest of your life. You can choose to make a change and to turn things around in your own life. You have the ability to do that now. You stop blaming other people so that you can get unstuck. They aren't the ones stuck, you are. They've moved on. Let go of your past. You can't move forward holding on to your past. Your past disappointments, your past failures, your past hurts; that's just what they are, they are the past. And when you spend time nurturing these hurts and nurturing these failures, you are preventing your future from happening.

You cannot be a victim and be victorious. You can either be a victim or you can be victorious, but you can't be both. You can have victory or you can remain a victim. You choose. You can make changes or you can make excuses, but you can't do both. You have to make a decision. You have to make a choice. What do you want to do? Do you want to be a victim or do you want to be victorious? Do you want a change in your life or are you just content making excuses and not going anywhere? These are things that you have to make a decision about. This is living life on purpose and making purposeful decisions about your life. Aren't you tired of feeling like your wheels are just spinning and you're not going anywhere? That's something that you have to decide for yourself and that you have total control of. You know that you have more to give, you know that you have more to do, you know that there is purpose, you know that there's destiny for your life. If you're going to get there you have to get to a place where you stop making excuses, stop blaming other people, and show up in your own life and make something happen. Get over your past and move forward. You can't live in your past and live in your future at the same time. You can't even move toward your future fully while being stuck in your past.

Here's the perfect example. Imagine you are walking along and the dress or jacket you are wearing gets stuck on a doorknob and it yanks you back. That's exactly what happens when you spend so much time in your past or making excuses. It's like you're going forward and you're going towards you're future and then something that you haven't dealt with properly will trigger within you to cause you to start thinking about your past and it just yanks you back. You are never going to reach your future that way. You are never going reach your destiny. You are never going to follow your dreams thinking about and holding on to your past. My challenge to you is to work through the issues of your past, move forward, forgive, don't look back, but just move forward, and look forward.

If anything, use your past and the pain of your past to help others and then take that pain and use it to make a profit instead of it torturing you for the rest of your life. When you do that, YOU win. Turn it for good! It's a must. If you're going to reach success in any area of your life, you must stop making excuses and you must stop blaming, and you must move forward on purpose.

You have so much to offer. You have so much potential on the inside of you. You want to make sure that you are maximizing all of your potential. Don't let it go to waste. Guess what? You owe yourself that much. AND there is somebody out there who is waiting on you to show up in your own life, so that you can help them get unstuck in his or her life.

Having Your Cake

CHAPTER 8
Don't Throw Away the Crumbs

When it seems like life has beaten you up and you've gone through so much, it seems like everyone else is prospering and doing well. They have a whole cake and all you have are crumbs. I want to encourage you – don't throw away the crumbs. There is value in the crumbs. If you've got nothing but crumbs, you have enough to get the job done. Sometimes you have to make it work with what you have until you can do better! And better only comes when you work what you have! Most people get stuck because they're looking for the something better without using what they already have to get better. Show your commitment to the lesser and you'll see the better!

When we talked about the ingredients in the cake and how you have all of them available to you, guess what? Whatever is in the cake is in the crumbs too. Trust me, you have everything you need. Don't give up on your dreams because you feel like you've given so much of yourself away to others that all you have left is crumbs. So what? The crumbs are good. Do you know people who love to eat the crumbs off a plate? Of course you do. Why do they eat the crumbs? Because the crumbs are still good and taste just like the cake. Everything that the cake has the crumb has. Yes you don't get the full pleasure of the cake, but you sure can tell if it was a good cake just by eating the crumbs. Don't throw away the crumbs.

Your faith and tenacity is being tested with the crumbs. I like to use Bible references and parables to help make my point and there's one that's perfect for this—Jesus and the Canaanite woman. There was a Canaanite woman, a gentile, who sought help for her demon-possessed daughter. She indicated that the effects were particularly cruel, but didn't give details. But it was recognized as something different than a physical illness. When the cause was physical, the Lord would say so. It is not true that they were just superstitious and thought every sickness was caused by evil spirits. But some were.

Jesus' disciples asked Him to send her away. They did not care much for Gentiles. Jesus explained to her that He was sent only to "the lost sheep of the house of Israel." This refers to His personal ministry on earth, that He had been sent to preach unto Israel. So, they tried to send her away but this woman would not give up. She persevered and refused to walk away without getting what she wanted. She was determined and begged, "Lord, help me." Jesus replied, "It is not good to take the children's bread (Israel) and throw it to the dogs (Gentiles)." What a stunning thing for Jesus to say! But there was a point to be made behind it all.

But just as stunning was her reply, "Yes, Lord; but even the dogs feed on the crumbs which fall from their master's table." It's as if she does not care about anything other than that this Prophet can help her daughter and she will not be dissuaded. A number of things happen at this point. First, the woman's faith is certainly tested. It will indeed take great courage and commitment to put up with this! This woman is going to learn something here. She is going to learn what a strong faith she has!

It would have been easy for her to turn away in anger or sorrow or pride. But she saw Jesus as the only hope for her daughter. She would not turn away! She wasn't leaving without getting what she wanted. That's how you have to be when you only have crumbs to work with. You have to believe that even with these crumbs you're going to get what you need. Just like the Canaanite woman didn't give up, you can't give up. Check out what happened because she was willing to work with just the crumbs.

Jesus answered, "O woman, your faith is great; be it done for you as you wish." Jesus certainly knew this about the woman's faith. Great faith brings great rewards. This took courage. It took commitment. It took a spirit that refused to be deterred. Her faith was tested and passed the test and the disciples received a lesson that they would remember.

Our faith needs to have endurance too. When that day was over, and this mother held her daughter in her arms, free at last from the cruel bondage she had suffered, and reflected on the events of that day, how do you think she felt? Jesus had pronounced her faith as "great". He had answered her request for her daughter's healing. She had not let the others persuade her to give up. She had haters. And in this instance Jesus' disciples were the haters. Do you know any of them? And, even at that darkest moment when it seemed as if she would not find the answer she desired, she pressed on. So, how did she feel at day's end? She had only asked for crumbs from the Master's table. She instead had received a feast. You can be sure she felt fine.

The feast is coming
Don't focus so much on the feast that you forget about the crumbs and count them as useless. Sometimes when we think big, and I'm not saying we shouldn't thing big. But, don't get paralyzed by the bigger. In other words you're so focused on the future and your desire for the future, that you stay stuck instead of working what you have until you get what you want. Now in no way am I suggesting that you be satisfied with crumbs. You should always want and strive for the whole cake. But the fact of the matter is, you have to start where you are and don't discount small beginnings.

Most self-made billionaires were not born billionaires. They were born like you and me but they desired to be exceptional. They wanted more than what they had and they believed it was possible. Sometimes, most people believe that billionaires such as Bill Gates and Mark Zuckerberg showed up overnight to become billionaires. That's definitely not true. Most of the billionaires today were what people would consider nobodies with just crumbs sometime ago but they started small and kept at it.

There are plenty of millionaires even billionaires who started with just the crumbs. Some of the wealthiest people today were dirt poor at one time. You could be the next rags to riches story. Did you know that Starbucks' Howard Schultz grew up in a housing complex for the poor? He grew up in the projects! In an interview with a British newspaper Schultz says: "Growing up I always felt like I was living on the other side of the tracks. I knew the people on the other side had more resources, more money, and happier families. And for some reason, I don't know why or how, I wanted to climb over that fence and achieve something beyond what people were saying was possible. I may have a suit and tie on now but I know where I'm from and I know what it's like." He now has a net worth of more than $2 billion.

Forever 21 founder Do Won Chang worked as a janitor, gas station attendant, and in a coffee shop when he first moved to America. He and his wife didn't always have it easy. After moving to America from Korea in 1981, Do Won worked those three jobs at the same time to make ends meet. They opened their first clothing store in 1984. Forever 21 is now an international, 480-store empire that rakes in around $3 billion in sales a year.

John Paul DeJoria, the man behind a hair-care empire, once lived in a foster home and his car. Before the age of 10 he sold Christmas cards and newspapers to help support his family. He was eventually was sent to live in a foster home and even spent some time in a gang before joining the military. With a $700 loan, DeJoria created John Paul Mitchell Systems and sold the shampoo door-to-door while living in his car. He's now worth more than $4 billion.

You see there is no excuse. If you have crumbs you have enough to do anything that you desire. Be persistent and never give up and don't throw away the crumbs. Your life is not over, you just may need to start over! And starting over is great because this time you get to create the life you want!

Power Affirmations:
- My past does not dictate my future.
- I have the faith and tenacity to turn my life around.

Power Practice:

1. Take inventory of what you do have and write everything down. What have you not lost yet? Do you still have a right mind? Do you still have your physical health? Do you still have a gift or talent?

Work with what you have and make it work for you.

2. Create a gratitude journal. This will help you to remember to always be thankful for what you do have. If you're not thankful for what you already have, why do you deserve more?

CHAPTER 9

Treat People Like Icing

When talking about having your cake and eat it too, your cake is your desired success or your desired result. It's what you really want in your life or business. You want to make sure that when you have gone through life, you've gone through whatever you've gone through that at the end of the day your desired success is what you have. You want to enjoy the fruit of your labor, you want to reap the benefits of your hard work and the trials and tribulations that you've gone through. You want to make sure that at the end you have the desired results that you want out of your life.

One thing that you have to realize is that when God made you he saw what He made and said, "yes, that is good, you are good". So, just like a good cake you have to understand that you have all the right ingredients, that's how you were made. You have access to everything you need to be successful in life because it's on the inside of you and it's just waiting for you to bring it all together. Just like a cake, you can have the ingredients, but if you have those ingredients in the cabinet or just on the shelf and you're not doing anything with them, you still don't have a cake. All you have are ingredients that you can't benefit from. Ingredients have to be brought together and mixed to perfection.

When you're preparing to bake a cake, you gather all of your ingredients, you blend them well and then you bake. It's a process. It's no different from you. You have the ingredients, however, you may need help identifying them if you don't know them, but once you've identified them you have to figure out how to blend these together to work for your benefit, to work for your life success. Once that's figured out you stand on what you know and then you go through the process. Sometimes the process is difficult because that's the heating process. Just like a cake you have to go into the heat and get baked. That is life's trials and tribulations that send you through that process and you have to make sure that you stay strong through the process because it's preparing you for your destiny and your dreams to manifest. They are waiting on you to arrive to your destination. They are waiting on you to complete the process, to complete the blending together, getting to know who you are and getting to know that you have what it takes, that you have the potential that you have it all inside of you.

The Icing on the Cake

Using the analogy of the cake. Have you ever had a really good cake? For example, my mom makes this awesome pound cake. I promise you it's the best pound cake this side of heaven. Sometimes when she makes it, she doesn't even put icing on it. She normally makes this little glaze, a light glaze that she puts on the pound cake, but sometimes she doesn't for whatever reason. The cake is still good. The icing is extra. The icing is optional. A good cake does not need icing. The icing is nice to have, you know, it gives it a little flavor or whatever, it gives it a little extra oomph, but guess what...even without the icing the cake is still good. So, that's what you have to realize about yourself. You are like that good cake and everyone in your life you have to make sure that their role in your life is icing. They are optional.

People cannot be a main ingredient in your life. Because if they're a main ingredient and they decide to exit your life for whatever reason or, God forbid, some unforeseen circumstance causes them to exit your life, if they were a main ingredient in your life then you fall apart. Just like in baking a cake, you have to have certain ingredients. You have to have flour, you have to have the egg, and you have to have the baking soda or baking powder. There are certain parts that you have to have in there. They are main ingredients. The icing is extra. So, you want to make sure that no one, outside of God himself is a main ingredient in your life. They have to be icing. You have to be in a place that you know that you are good, that you are complete, that you are whole. You are good all by yourself. Anything else, is icing on the cake. It's extra and it's optional.

So, when you have a relationship in your life and it falls apart for whatever reason, it's just like scraping that icing off the cake. You just scrape it off and keep it moving. Keep it moving because they were just icing. You're not going to fall apart. Now, the other part of that though is you have to even be careful of who you allow to be icing, because although you can scrape the icing off, it still causes some damage to the cake. So, never let anyone be a main ingredient, put them in the role of icing, but still be careful of who you allow to be icing in your life.

This is something that you really have to grab a hold of if you want to have your cake and eat it too. No matter what area of your life it is, whether it's relationships, even if it's a business relationship you have to be careful of how you allow people to interact with you. You must go into any relationship confident of your ability for success and that your success is not tied to that person, because if something happens to that relationship, whether business or personal, and that person decides to bail you have to know that you can still be successful without that person. That person and that business relationship are simply icing. They're not and can never be a main ingredient.

Many times we as women get so caught up in relationships this way. Because our confidence level and self-esteem level isn't as strong as it should be, we enter romantic relationship giving the man a main ingredient role. We turn over so much to that person and sometimes without even giving him the opportunity to earn it. That is not healthy. Understand that you can have a great and committed relationship while designating your relationship as icing. I've seen so many women who go into depression, lose hope, all but give up on relationships all together simply because they allowed one man to be in a role he wasn't even designed for—main ingredient.

Even if you're married, you husband is not a main ingredient. He is icing. He should compliment who you already are. You become just a little bit tastier with him, but you're just as good without him. And yes, even your children are icing. Why, because they will always be your children but they will not always be in your life in the same way. When they become adults, you have to know that you are still good. Do you know any women who once their children became adults and began lives and families of their own independent of their parents, they just fall apart? This is because they allowed their child or children to have main ingredient roles. Our children are basically on loan to us. We invest in them, do the best we can and pray that we get a return on our investment with their success. However, parenting your child comes to an end. Your children are icing. Your job is not a main ingredient. You can be so consumed working a career that you allow it take an inappropriate role in your life. You work from sun up until sun down, for someone else, to help build their dreams. But what happens when it's time for budget cuts and your name is on the list? I promise you, you are not a main ingredient for them. You are just icing and they have no problem letting you go.

Know that you are enough. There isn't a person, a job, a career, or relationship that can make you more whole than how God created you to be.

So, it doesn't matter what part of your life it is, you have to make sure that people are assigned the role of icing. They are optional. Using this concept makes your life so much easier. It adds a little more peace to your life. This is how I make this work for me. Someone could be in your life and they could be giving you hard time about something and you could be just going through all kinds of problems with them, but while they're there, in your face or whatever they're doing, just say to them in your mind, "you know what, you are just icing. I'm not going to let you stress me out today. You are just icing; and if you decide to get out of dodge, it's okay, because I'm good all by myself. "

I am good! Just like a good baked cake! I am good!

CHAPTER 10

Brand You New

One of the most important things you can do to totally change your life and create the life that you really want is to create what's known as a personal brand. Everything about you should be intentional. YOU are a brand whether you own it or not. What message are you sending? Using the information I've provided in the first nine chapters, along with the tips I'm going to give you now about how to create a personal brand will catapult your life and business to another dimension. Are you ready?

The first thing I want you to know is that branding is not just for business. It's not just for big business like Coke, Pepsi, or Nike. Branding is not just for small business. Branding is a necessity if you want to live your dream life. You have to stand out for something. Whether it's starting a business or working for someone else, if you're going to be successful you have to stand out and be known for something. Personal branding helps you control what you're known for and how other people perceive you. Perception is reality even when it comes to what people think of you. When you are out of touch with who you are and what you represent, it makes you vulnerable and more prone to have your brand defined for you by others.

If you're sending out the wrong messages or mixed messages, it's going to hinder your level of success. You have value and you add value but you have to be intentional about focusing on it so that you build the personal brand that you want, so that you create the one you want?

Aren't you tired of being behind the scenes and watching countless others accomplish so much more? You watch them and they may be doing something similar to what you'd like to do and you think to yourself, "They're not even that good, I can do it better." And guess what? You're probably right. But here's what they're doing right, they've created a brand for themselves and began to market themselves as that brand. You just keep thinking and talking about what you're going to do, but no action follows.

Branding Increases Your Value
Put some water, some sugar, and some fizz in a can and the cost is about 10 cents. Put Coca Cola on that can and the price just jumped up to $1.25. It's all about the brand. You know from personal experience that "brand" name items cost more. Well technically, all names are a "brand" name but how much value is with that name makes the

difference. This is why it's important to be intentional about your brand. You have one whether you own it or not, but is it Wal-mart or couture?

The Three Ps of Personal Branding

Purpose
Your name has meaning. When someone thinks of your name, they have some predisposed thoughts about you—who you are, what you do, and how you do it.

- Are you the go to person for something?
- What are you really good at?
- Are you the pain in the behind?
- Are you the Mrs. (or Mr.) Negative?
- Are you the one that's always complaining?
- Are you the one who's always borrowing money, so people hate to see you coming?

I want you to think about that for a moment. There are thoughts attached to your name and if you're going to be a success, you should be concerned with those thoughts that you are contributing to. I'm not one that believes in caring too much about what others think of you, because if you're overly sensitive it can impact your confidence level. However, when it comes to creating a personal brand and creating the type of life you want, knowing what the perception is about you is important. Some of what people think of you is because of their internal issues, but some of what they think is because of what you're putting out there. You can't control other people's issues, but you can and must be intentional about what you're putting out.

Multiple streams of YOU
What does your name say in the social media arena? When your posts show up on someone's wall are they scrolling past as fast as they can to avoid seeing or reading what you've posted? Do you have social media multiple personality disorder? One day your mood is up and you're encouraging everybody and then the next day you're down and telling everybody off. One day you're closing down your Facebook page, the next day you're posting all day long. Make up your mind about whom you're going to be. Your social media presence is a direct reflection of what you have going on internally.

No matter how hard you try to hide it, the truth always comes out in your social media conversations. If your Facebook wall is messy with a lot of drama because you've connected with people who perpetrate low value, that's a good indication that your personal life is messy and filled with drama and your circle is filled with people who perpetrate low value. It always amazes me when people complain about what they see on their own Facebook wall. You are in control of whom you are connected to on social media. It doesn't matter what platform that you're using. If someone does not have your same values, purpose, and interests then do not connect with them. If you're already connected, then disconnect. It will not be the end of the world if you unfriend someone, even if it's family. Just because they're "family" does not give them a special pass to make your life miserable! Love them from a distance!

If you work a job, you have a brand there. If you're an entrepreneur, you have a brand with your clients. They have very specific thoughts about you and in both cases those thoughts translate to value and dictate what you're worth to them. When it comes time to make job cuts, you don't want to be the one branded as always coming in late, or the one who is insubordinate, or the one who does just enough to get by. When you create your personal brand and infuse who you are or desire to be known for into your job, career, or business you will increase your value and command higher income potential. People gravitate to those who stand for something and have a clear value to what they bring to the table.

Know what's on your plate. What can you bring to the table that nobody else can offer? If someone else can bring something similar, how can you do it differently? You can put your spin on it; bring your uniqueness and own it.

Personality

Whatever brand you desire to create, the most important thing you have to do for lasting success is to stay within your personality. Be authentic in who you're presenting.

Fakeness can only last so long. Whether it's in business or your personal life. How long do you think you can keep the facade going? Eventually the real you will come out.

So, instead of trying to pretend to be someone you're not, just be yourself from the get-go. Faking takes up too much energy and that energy can be better spent working on the real you and getting real results.

Whatever your personality, you can make it work for you. That part of you that you've been hiding, could be the very thing that sets you apart and increases your value in your business. Stop trying to conform based on other people's expectations. Trying to fit into a box that wasn't designed to hold you will keep you stuck and broke. Instead, use your uniqueness to accentuate your value and come out of the box. It will give you a peace of mind, less stress, and freedom just to be.

Presence

How do you present yourself? This is similar to personality but presence is the image that you are projecting, or think you are projecting, and may or may not align with how other people see you.

When focused on creating a brand, your image is what can seal the deal for you. The image that you're portraying should align completely with your personality and in business with the type of personalities you want to attract as clients. For example, if your personality is creative, extroverted, energetic and quirky then you mostly likely aren't attracted to black, white, and grayscale colors. If your ideal client has that personality, then you do not want those colors as part of your brand colors because they would be lifeless to your client.

What tends to happen is that we have a perception of how we "should" do things based on what others are doing and so we conform. You may feel that to be more professional you should wear dark suits or clothing. Here's the thing. If your personality doesn't match, you look and seem awkward. And, your ideal clients will not be attracted to you because there will be a disconnect. Vibrant colors are just as professional as dark or monochrome colors. It depends on your brand and whom you want to attract.

Everything about your image should speak to who you want to be as a brand. If you're in business, then that includes whom you want to attract as a client. If it's your career, then it's based on what career you want. If it's a relationship, then your image should reflect who you want to attract. Image is everything.

Your conversations and your relationships are also part of your image. Again, consider who you are as a brand and what image is being relayed through your conversation (in person and social media).

If there's a disconnect between your personality and your image, then that calls for reflection. Are you really being authentic or are you fitting in to someone else's expectations. When you always have to reign in who you are because you're concerned about what someone else will say or feel about your true personality, then that is an indication that you're not being authentic. And when you're not being authentic, you're most likely not happy. Get to happy, and just be you. If those you're in relationship with cannot accept the real you then it's time to look at the real value of those relationships. Always remember to love yourself first and more than you love someone else.

Your New Success Starts Now

Are you prepared, right now, to start living the life of success that you really want? If you implement the advice in this book, you will be well on your way. This is just a beginning.

Every opportunity is before you to start creating the life you want. No better time exists than right now for you to work on making it happen. Look, nothing changes if nothing changes. It starts and ends with you and what you're going to do from this moment forward.

You already have everything you need available to you to make it happen, but the question is-- what are you doing to do about it?

ABOUT THE AUTHOR

An innovative business coach, entrepreneur, empowerment speaker and author, Cheryl is the founder of A'Sista Project—an empowerment haven for savvy, sassy, smart women who want to have their cake and eat it too in business & life! A'Sista Project's focus is to increase the social, economic, and spiritual strength of women by developing confidence and building life and business success. She does this through private and group coaching, seminars, workshops, and conferences.

As a branding connoisseur, Cheryl works with entrepreneurs, speakers, authors, consultants and coaches to build their brands and turn their websites into money making profit centers through her branding and design company, A'Sista Media Group, LLC. Her business coaching clients look to her for help attracting more clients, expanding their influence and increasing their income.

Cheryl is the host of an annual event, Permission Granted Empowerment Seminar where she brings together other empowering women to help motivate and inspire attendees to greatness. She is the creator of the Make It Happen Business Boot Camp, an 8-week business training program and the Idea to Income Formula home study program.

To learn more about Cheryl, visit www.asistaproject.com

www.ingramcontent.com/pod-product-compliance
Lightning Source LLC
Chambersburg PA
CBHW060610100426
42744CB00008B/1381